D1326469

GRAPHIC MYSTERIES
ATLANTIS
AND OTHER LOST CITIES
by Rob Shone
illustrated by Jim Eldridge

BOOK   HOUSE

Designed and produced by
David West Children's Books
7 Princeton Court
55 Felsham Road
London SW15 1AZ

Editors: Charlotte Cattermole, Kate Newport

Photo credits:
Page 4, NASA; Page 5, Dan Brandenburg/iStockphoto.com; Page 45, Michael
Owen/iStockphoto.com

First published in 2006 by **Book House**,
an imprint of **The Salariya Book Company Ltd**
25 Marlborough Place, Brighton BN1 1UB

Please visit the Salariya Book Company at:
www.salariya.com

HB ISBN 1 905087 83 7
PB ISBN 1 905087 84 5

Visit our website at **www.book-house.co.uk**
for free electronic versions of:
You Wouldn't Want to Be an Egyptian Mummy!
You Wouldn't Want to Be a Roman Gladiator!
Avoid joining Shackleton's Polar Expedition!

A catalogue record for this book is available from the British Library.
Printed on paper from sustainable forests.

Manufactured in China.

CONTENTS

HIDDEN PLACES

People have told stories of lost civilisations and their ancient cities for thousands of years. The mystery surrounding these lost cities still divides experts today. Did they exist at all? Where could they have been, and how did they vanish?

There are still many ancient sites waiting to be explored in Central America, such as this pre-Colombian ruin in modern-day Costa Rica.

ATLANTIS – It was the philosopher Plato who first described this beautiful but doomed city, in c. 400 B.C. Since then, historians and treasure seekers have tried to find out where Atlantis is and how it was destroyed. So far they have all failed.

EL DORADO – This is a legendary golden city believed to have been in South America. It is linked to stories of an ancient king, also named 'El Dorado' (Spanish for 'The Golden Man'), who covered himself in gold.

CAMELOT – Camelot is the legendary court of King Arthur. There are many theories about where in Great Britain it might have been, but there is still no hard evidence to prove that it existed at all.

Mu – A lost paradise known as Mu was once thought to have been the Garden of Eden from the Bible. Experts believe that Mu was destroyed by a natural disaster, such as an earthquake or flood. Some claim that the Pacific Islands are all that remains of Mu.

THE KINGDOM OF PRESTER JOHN – This legendary kingdom was ruled over by a Christian priest-king called Prester John. His kingdom was said to contain the fountain of life, and all John's subjects were happy, healthy, and peaceful. However, the legend also states that this paradise was almost impossible to reach.

LYONESSE – Connected to tales of King Arthur, Lyonesse was once a country beyond Land's End in Cornwall, England. Legend says that a great storm blew up, and the sea covered the land. When Arthur returns however, Lyonesse will again rise from the ocean waters.

OGYGIA – Ogygia was the island of the goddess Calypso, a figure in Greek mythology. It was very cold, and full of dark forests and scary beasts. Calpyso kept the hero Odysseus here for many years.

This Inca city was discovered at the top of Machu Picchu at the beginning of the twentieth century. Nobody knows what happened to the people who once lived there.

LOST CITIES

Explorers and scientists have searched all over the world to find anything that could lead to the discovery of these legendary lost cities. Historical writings, myths, folk tales, and artefacts all leave clues to where such places may be found.

A CITY BENEATH THE SEA
Plato first told the story of how Atlantis was destroyed. He described it as being located on a large island in the ocean west of the Pillars of Hercules. Since then, evidence of past civilisations that may have been Atlantis, such as human bones and tools, have been found in places around the world, including near Thera, Greece, and off the west coast of Cuba.

GREECE

Thera

① CRETE

MEDITERRANEAN SEA

FLORIDA

BAHAMAS

②

Bimini Islands

CUBA

④

①

②

③

A world map showing the locations of the smaller maps.

6

TREASURE HUNT

In 1541, a party of Conquistadors, led by the Spaniard Gonzalo Pizzaro, set out on an expedition deep into the heart of the Amazon. They were searching for El Dorado, a city of gold that Indians said existed hidden in the jungle. When Orellana returned to Spain, he brought with him amazing tales of a lost civilisation packed with riches. For 500 years, explorers have searched for El Dorado.

Inca gold cup

③

④

MEDIEVAL MYSTERY

The legend of King Arthur and his medieval court at Camelot is known throughout the world. It tells of how a powerful and holy king, along with his chivalrous Knights of the Round Table, united his people and defeated evil. However, nobody really knows whether Arthur or Camelot actually existed. Even so, many places still claim to have been the site of Camelot.

This map of Great Britain shows some of the places where Camelot might have been.

ATLANTIS

SEPTEMBER 1968. LOCAL FISHING GUIDE, 'BONEFISH' SAM ELLIS, DROPPED HIS ANCHOR. HIS FLAT-BOTTOMED SKIFF FLOATED IN THE SHALLOWS OFF THE WEST COAST OF BIMINI, AN ISLAND IN THE BAHAMAS...

HE WAS MORE USED TO TAKING TOURISTS OUT ON FISHING TRIPS. BUT TODAY HIS PASSENGER WAS INTERESTED IN SOMETHING OTHER THAN FISHING.

LET ME GET THIS RIGHT, DOC — I'VE BROUGHT YOU ALL THE WAY OUT HERE JUST SO YOU CAN LOOK AT SOME *OLD STONES*?

...IF WHAT PEOPLE HAVE TOLD ME ABOUT THEM IS TRUE, THOSE OLD STONES MIGHT BE VALUABLE.

I'M AN ARCHAEOLOGIST, BONEFISH. IT'S MY JOB TO LOOK AT OLD STONES. BESIDES...

I'LL SEE YOU IN ABOUT TWENTY MINUTES.

SPLOOOSH!!

DR. MASON VALENTINE DISAPPEARED...

...BENEATH THE DARK BLUE WATERS.

SUDDENLY...

ATLANTIS – ISLAND HOME OF POSEIDON, THE GOD OF THE SEA. POSEIDON FELL IN LOVE WITH CLEITO, A HUMAN, AND BUILT THE CITY OF ATLANTIS FOR HER.

ON A HILL AT THE CENTRE OF THE CITY STOOD THE TEMPLE OF POSEIDON.

HERE, THE TEN SONS OF CLEITO WORSHIPPED THEIR FATHER AND RULED WISELY OVER THE ISLAND.

THE CENTRE OF THE CITY WAS CIRCLED BY THREE CANALS AND BY THREE GREAT WALLS. A FOURTH CANAL LINKED THEM ALL TO THE SEA.

TEMPLE OF POSEIDON

INNER CANAL

OUTER CANAL

CANAL TO SEA

OUTSIDE THE THIRD WALL...

...WERE THE HOUSES AND MARKETS OF THE PEOPLE OF ATLANTIS.

BEYOND THE CITY LAY A FERTILE PLAIN THAT STRETCHED TO THE DISTANT MOUNTAINS.

NO MATTER WHAT TIME OF YEAR, THERE WAS ALWAYS ENOUGH FOOD FOR EVERYONE. FROM THE VERY SMALL...

...TO THE VERY LARGE.

THE ROCKS OF ATLANTIS WERE RICH IN PRECIOUS METALS AND GEMS. THE ATLANTEANS BECAME WEALTHY BY TRADING WITH THEIR NEIGHBOURS.

MEANWHILE, ZEUS, RULER OF THE GODS, SAW HOW EVIL AND CORRUPT THE PEOPLE OF ATLANTIS HAD BECOME. HE DECIDED THAT THEY MUST BE *PUNISHED*.

ONE TERRIBLE DAY AND NIGHT, THE GODS CAUSED THE WATERS AROUND ATLANTIS TO RISE. THE ISLAND WAS SWALLOWED BY THE FURIOUS WAVES OF THE SEA.

WHEN MORNING CAME, ATLANTIS HAD VANISHED.

SO, AFTER BEING LOST UNDER THE WAVES FOR NEARLY 12,000 YEARS, HAD DR. VALENTINE AND BONEFISH SAM FINALLY FOUND ATLANTIS IN THE CARRIBEAN? SOME PEOPLE PLACE ATLANTIS MUCH CLOSER TO GREECE, ON THE ISLAND OF THERA (NOW CALLED SANTORINI), IN THE MEDITERRANEAN SEA.

LONG BEFORE PLATO'S TIME, A MIGHTY CIVILISATION GREW ON THE MEDITERRANEAN ISLAND OF CRETE –THE MINOANS. SEA TRADE HAD MADE THE MINOANS WEALTHY, AND THEIR CITIES AND PALACES WERE THE MARVEL OF THEIR AGE.

THERA, WAS A LIVELY MINOAN COLONY. ON ITS STEEP-SIDED AND FERTILE SLOPES WERE MINOAN SETTLEMENTS, VILLAGES, AND A ROYAL PALACE.

AT THE ISLAND'S HEART, THOUGH, WAS A VOLCANO. IT HAD BEEN DORMANT FOR MANY YEARS – BUT IT WAS ABOUT TO **AWAKEN AGAIN!**

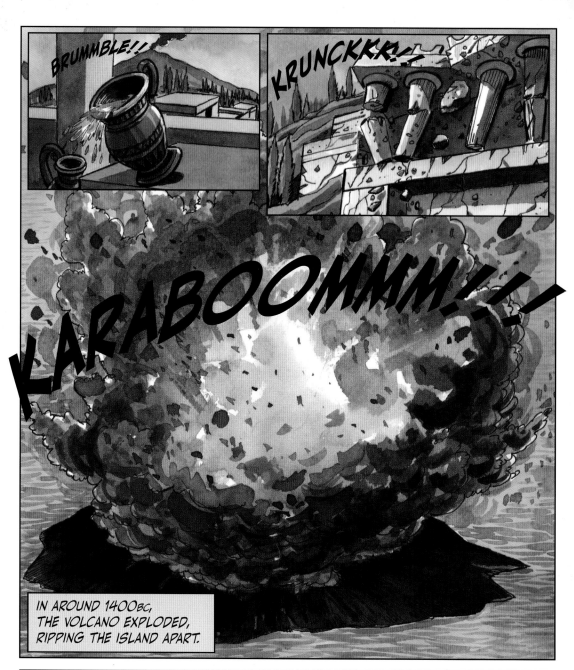

IN AROUND 1400BC,
THE VOLCANO EXPLODED,
RIPPING THE ISLAND APART.

THE EXPLOSION CAUSED
EARTHQUAKES AND A TIDAL
WAVE THAT THUNDERED
TOWARD NEARBY ISLANDS,
INCLUDING CRETE. THE
MINOAN CIVILISATION NEVER
RECOVERED FROM THE
DEVASTATION. IN A FEW
YEARS IT HAD DISAPPEARED
ENTIRELY. COULD THERA,
OR EVEN CRETE, HAVE
BEEN ATLANTIS?

MANY PEOPLE HAVE CLAIMED TO KNOW WHERE ATLANTIS IS. PLACING IT EVERYWHERE FROM THE JUNGLES OF SOUTH AMERICA...

...TO THE ICY WASTELANDS OF THE ANTARCTIC.

PERHAPS ATLANTIS WAS NEVER MORE THAN A LEGEND.

YET PEOPLE STILL HOPE THAT ITS RUINS LIE HIDDEN SOMEWHERE, JUST WAITING TO BE FOUND...

THE END

EL DORADO

IN APRIL 1925, COLONEL PERCY HARRISON FAWCETT LEFT CUIBÁ, IN BRAZIL, AND WALKED INTO THE DENSE MATTO GROSSO JUNGLE OF SOUTH AMERICA.

WITH HIM WERE HIS YOUNG SON, JACK, AND JACK'S FRIEND, RALEIGH RIMELL.

FAWCETT HAD HEARD MANY STRANGE TALES OVER THE YEARS OF ANCIENT RUINS, CRUMBLING IN THE DARK HEART OF THE JUNGLE.

BUT ONE STORY SEEMED DIFFERENT. IT TOLD OF A SECRET CITY, FULL OF RICHES AND WEALTH, A CITY OF MYSTERY – AND FAWCETT BELIEVED HE KNEW WHERE IT WAS. HE CALLED IT CITY 'Z.'

WHAT WAS CITY 'Z'? COULD FAWCETT AND HIS PARTY HAVE BEEN SEARCHING FOR THE LOST CITY OF EL DORADO?

FAWCETT THOUGHT THEY WOULD BE GONE FOR FEWER THAN TWO YEARS. HE WAS MISTAKEN - THEY WERE NEVER SEEN AGAIN.

NO ONE KNOWS WHAT HAPPENED TO FAWCETT, HIS SON, OR RALEIGH RIMELL. HAD THE LEGEND OF EL DORADO CLAIMED THREE MORE LIVES?

WHERE DID THE LEGEND OF EL DORADO BEGIN? IN 1531, THE SPANIARD, FRANCISCO PIZARRO, LEADING 177 MEN, LANDED ON THE WESTERN COAST OF SOUTH AMERICA. IN JUST A FEW MONTHS THIS SMALL BAND OF SOLDIERS CONQUERED THE MIGHTY INCA EMPIRE.

THE INCA COULD NOT RESIST THE SPANISH FIREARMS.

THE INCA KING, ATAHUALPA, WAS CAPTURED AND HELD FOR RANSOM BY PIZARRO. THE SPANIARDS SET THE PRICE FOR HIS RELEASE...

HAVE YOU EVER SEEN SO MUCH GOLD IN ONE PLACE BEFORE?! **A WHOLE ROOM** FILLED FROM FLOOR TO CEILING WITH IT!

AND THERE ARE TWO MORE FILLED WITH SILVER! IT'S NOT ENOUGH TO SAVE THEIR KING FROM THE EXECUTIONER, THOUGH.

WHERE DO YOU THINK IT ALL CAME FROM?

I DON'T KNOW, BUT I BET YOU THERE'S MORE TREASURE OUT THERE.

THE INCA ARE CLEVER. I THINK THIS IS JUST A FRACTION OF THEIR GOLD. THEY'VE HIDDEN THE REST IN THE MOUNTAINS OR IN THE JUNGLE.

SOON, RUMOURS SPREAD THROUGHOUT THE SPANISH CAMP...

THE INCA CALL IT MANOA, AN ENTIRE CITY OF GOLD, RULED BY A GOLDEN KING.

THE WALLS OF THE BUILDINGS ARE MADE OF SOLID GOLD, AND THE STREETS ARE PAVED WITH INGOTS OF PURE SILVER.

EVEN EVERYDAY THINGS – SPOONS, PLATES, CUPS – ARE ALL MADE OF GOLD.

SO WHERE IS THIS CITY OF GOLD?

I DON'T KNOW, BUT THE INCA DO, AND THEY CAN BE **MADE** TO TELL US EXACTLY WHERE IT IS!

THE SPANISH LUSTED AFTER THIS TREASURE. THEY CALLED THE GOLDEN CITY EL DORADO, AND THEY MEANT TO FIND IT!

BY 1539, THE SPANISH HAD BROUGHT THE WHOLE INCA EMPIRE UNDER THEIR CONTROL. AT QUITO, A TOWN TO THE NORTH OF SPAIN'S NEW TERRITORY, 1541...

WHAT'S HAPPENING DOWN THERE?

IT'S THE NEW GOVERNOR. HE AND SOME OF HIS MEN ARE GOING OFF TO FIND OUT WHAT'S ON THE OTHER SIDE OF THE MOUNTAINS TO THE EAST.

THE NEW GOVERNOR OF QUITO WAS GONZALO, YOUNGER BROTHER OF FRANCISCO PIZARRO.

HE CHOSE HIS FRIEND AND COUSIN, FRANCISCO DE ORELLANA, AS HIS SECOND IN COMMAND. THEIR MISSION WAS TO FIND EL DORADO.

IN FEBRUARY 1541, THE LARGE EXPEDITION LEFT QUITO FOR THE FOOTHILLS OF THE ANDES.

THEY MADE GOOD PROGRESS AT FIRST...

WHAT ARE YOUR PLANS, GONZALO?

THE NATIVES SPEAK OF A SACRED WATERFALL NEARBY. ATAHUALPA'S GOLD IS THERE! I AM SURE OF IT.

THEY FOUND THE WATERFALL...

SO, THE TREASURE'S NOT HERE AFTER ALL.

NO. THE WATERFALL GUARDS ATAHUALPA'S SPIRIT, NOT HIS GOLD. LET'S MOVE ON.

25

IN THE MOUNTAINS, THEIR JOURNEY BECAME HARDER.

SIX MONTHS LATER, EAST OF THE MOUNTAINS...

NOTHING! JUST ENDLESS JUNGLE AS FAR AS THE EYE CAN SEE.

WELL, EL DORADO'S NOT HERE EITHER!

THE NATIVE GUIDES ARE DYING, SOON IT WILL BE OUR TURN.

THEY HAD BIGGER WORRIES, HOWEVER. THEIR FOOD WAS RUNNING OUT.

GONZALO! WE MUST TURN BACK! THERE IS NO FOOD HERE. THIS IS JUST A BARREN WASTELAND.

I WILL NOT BE DEFEATED, FRANCISCO! ORDER THE MEN TO BUTCHER THE HORSES. WE WILL EAT THEM UNTIL WE FIND FOOD, FURTHER ON.

THE SPANIARDS BUILT A RAFT TO CARRY THE SICK AND THEIR SUPPLIES. THE EXPEDITION SLOWLY MADE ITS WAY DOWN THE COCA RIVER.

AFTER A MONTH, GONZALO DECIDED TO STOP. THERE WERE FEW NATIVES LEFT ALIVE NOW, AND THE SPANIARDS HAD STARTED TO DIE AS WELL. THE MEN WERE CLOSE TO MUTINY.

FRANCISCO, I WANT YOU TO TAKE THE BOAT AND THE STRONGEST MEN. TRAVEL DOWN THE RIVER AND FIND FOOD. YOU'RE OUR LAST HOPE FOR SURVIVAL.

ON CHRISTMAS DAY, 1541, FRANCISO AND FIFTY-SEVEN MEN, LEFT PIZARRO AND DRIFTED DOWN THE COCA RIVER.

I'LL BE BACK IN TWO WEEKS.

FROM THE COCA RIVER, FRANCISCO ENTERED THE LARGER NAPO RIVER...

THE CURRENT IS TOO FAST AND STRONG! WE'LL NEVER BE ABLE TO GET BACK TO GONZALO. WE HAVE NO CHOICE BUT TO GO DOWNRIVER.

AFTER MANY DAYS, THE RIVER WIDENED AND THE CURRENT SLOWED. FRANCISCO'S MEN WERE STARVING, BUT THEY HAD REACHED THE AMAZON RAIN FOREST – AND FOOD!

LOOK!

QUICK! KILL IT SOMEONE!

MEANWHILE, BACK ON THE COCA RIVER, GONZALO WAS WAITING. HIS FOOD WAS ALMOST GONE, ALONG WITH HIS DREAM OF FINDING EL DORADO.

COMMANDER, IT'S BEEN MORE THAN TWO WEEKS NOW. FRANCISCO DE ORELLANA IS NOT COMING BACK. WHAT SHALL WE DO?

COMMANDER?

FRANCISCO, YOU WERE MY FRIEND! WHY HAVE YOU DESERTED ME? I SHALL HAVE MY REVENGE!

WE WILL GO BACK TO QUITO.

A FEW HUNDRED MILES TO THE EAST, FRANCISCO LIKE GONZALO, HAD ABANDONED HOPE OF FINDING THE GOLDEN CITY.

HIS BOAT DRIFTED SLOWLY DOWN THE NAPO RIVER...

...UNTIL IT REACHED THE MIGHTY AMAZON RIVER.

WHILE GONZALO PIZARRO STRUGGLED BACK TO QUITO, FRANCISCO HAD BUILT A BIGGER BOAT...

...AND WAS SAILING DOWN THE AMAZON.

LOOK! A CITY IN THE JUNGLE!

HAVE WE FOUND EL DORADO?

IF WE HAVE, THE NATIVES MEAN TO KEEP THEIR GOLD! DEFEND YOURSELVES!

ALL ALONG THE AMAZON THE TRIBES WERE HOSTILE.

EVENTUALLY, IN AUGUST 1542...

WHERE HAS THE OTHER RIVER BANK GONE? I CAN'T SEE IT.

THE WATER! IT'S SALTY!

WE'VE REACHED THE SEA!

ALTHOUGH FRANCISCO DE ORELLANA AND HIS MEN HAD NOT FOUND EL DORADO, THEY HAD BECOME THE FIRST EUROPEANS TO TRAVEL DOWN THE AMAZON TO ITS MOUTH. GONZALO PIZARRO'S WAS ONE OF THE LAST EXPEDITIONS MADE BY THE SPANISH TO FIND EL DORADO, THE CITY. THEY NOW BECAME INTERESTED IN EL DORADO, THE MAN...

LAKE GUATAVITA, NEAR BOGOTA, IN COLOMBIA.

THE SPANISH LEARNED THAT EACH YEAR, THE KING OF THE LOCAL CHIBCHA PEOPLE, COVERED FROM HEAD TO TOE IN GOLD DUST, WAS ROWED OUT TO THE MIDDLE OF THE LAKE.

GOLD OFFERINGS WERE MADE BY THE KING AND THE WATCHING CROWDS.

FINALLY, THE KING WASHED OFF THE GOLD DUST.

IN 1580, DON ANTONIO SEPULVEDA FOUND LAKE GUATAVITA.

THINK OF ALL THE GOLD THAT MUST LIE AT THE LAKE'S BOTTOM!

CAMELOT

A FIFTH-CENTURY A.D. MONASTERY IN BRITAIN...

??!

THE ROMAN LEGIONS THAT HAD OCCUPIED BRITAIN FOR SO LONG HAD FINALLY GONE. BUT THEY HAD LEFT THE COUNTRY DEFENCELESS. GERMANIC TRIBES FROM THE EUROPEAN MAINLAND SAW THEIR CHANCE.

ANGLES, SAXONS, AND JUTES MOVED WEST, DESTROYING THE MONASTERIES AND THE KNOWLEDGE AND LEARNING THEY POSSESSED. HISTORIES WERE LOST, AND CURRENT EVENTS WENT UNRECORDED. BECAUSE OF THE DESTRUCTION OF BOOKS AND MANUSCRIPTS CONTAINING SO MUCH KNOWLEDGE...

...THIS ERA BECAME KNOWN AS THE DARK AGES.

FLWHOOOSH!

THE INVADERS MOVED FROM PLACE TO PLACE, BURNING CHURCHES AND MONASTERIES WHEREVER THEY FOUND THEM. BUT THEN, STRANGELY, THEIR MARCH WEST SLOWED, AND FINALLY STOPPED.

LEGENDS SAY THAT ONE MAN WAS RESPONSIBLE FOR TURNING BACK THE ANGLO-SAXON INVASION. A GREAT KING UNITED THE PEOPLE AND STOOD AGAINST THE FOREIGN ENEMY, WINNING BATTLE AFTER BATTLE.

HE WAS ARTHUR, KING OF THE BRITONS. THE FINAL VICTORY CAME AT MOUNT BADON. THERE, MORE THAN 900 WESTERN SAXONS FELL BENEATH ARTHUR'S LEGENDARY SWORD, EXCALIBUR.

EVERY KING NEEDS A CASTLE — AND ARTHUR'S WAS CALLED CAMELOT.

FROM CAMELOT, THE KING AND HIS QUEEN, GUINEVERE, RULED THE LAND.

TO HELP HIM GOVERN AND DEFEND THE KINGDOM, ARTHUR FORMED A COUNCIL OF KNIGHTS — THE KNIGHTS OF THE ROUND TABLE.

FOR ADVICE, ARTHUR WOULD TURN TO MERLIN, THE MAGICIAN.

FOR MANY YEARS ARTHUR RULED THE LAND WISELY. HIS KNIGHTS SPENT THEIR TIME JOUSTING...

ERLANNNGG!

...OR RIDING OUT TO HELP THE PEOPLE IN TIMES OF TROUBLE.

BUT ARTHUR HAD ENEMIES AT COURT. HIS SON, MORDRED, WAS JEALOUS OF ARTHUR'S POWER AND POPULARITY. MORDRED PLOTTED AND TURNED THE KNIGHTS AGAINST ONE ANOTHER... SOON THERE WAS CIVIL WAR.

THE CIVIL WAR ENDED AT THE RIVER CAMLANN. THERE, ARTHUR FOUGHT HIS FINAL BATTLE. AS MOST OF THE KNIGHTS FROM BOTH SIDES LAY DEAD AND DYING, ARTHUR KILLED MORDRED. BUT IN DOING SO, HE HIMSELF WAS FATALLY WOUNDED.

WITH ARTHUR GONE, CAMELOT SOON BECAME A FAINT MEMORY, MORE LEGEND THAN HISTORY.

1969, CADBURY CASTLE, SOMERSET. THE CASTLE WAS AN OLD IRON-AGE FORT DATING BACK 5,000 YEARS. LOCAL LEGEND TOLD OF IT BEING THE SITE OF THE CASTLE AT CAMELOT.

LESLEY ALCOCK, HEAD OF THE CAMELOT RESEARCH COMMITTEE, WAS OVERSEEING AN ARCHAEOLOGICAL DIG THERE.

YOU CAN SEE THAT THE SOIL IS MADE UP OF LAYERS, LIKE A CAKE. EACH LAYER IS FROM A DIFFERENT PERIOD OF TIME.

BY LOOKING CAREFULLY AT THE PIECES OF BROKEN POTTERY IN THE LAYERS, WE CAN DATE EACH PERIOD.

WHAT THEY FOUND SURPRISED THEM. CADBURY CASTLE HAD BEEN MUCH BIGGER THAN PREVIOUSLY BELIEVED. IT WOULD HAVE TAKEN NEARLY 1,000 MEN TO DEFEND IT.

BUT THIS IS THE INTERESTING LAYER. IT DATES FROM THE END OF THE FIFTH CENTURY – KING ARTHUR'S TIME.

HAD LESLEY ALCOCK FOUND CAMELOT?

IT'S FROM THE RIGHT PERIOD, AND IT'S LARGE ENOUGH TO HAVE BEEN AN IMPORTANT DEFENSIVE STRONGHOLD.

IT WOULDN'T HAVE LOOKED LIKE THE CAMELOT OF LEGEND, THOUGH.

CADBURY CASTLE, C.490 A.D.

THE CELTIC TRIBES OF THE SOUTHWEST HAD ALWAYS BEEN MIGHTY. EVEN THE ROMANS FOUND THEM HARD TO CONTROL. WHEN THE ROMANS LEFT, IT WAS AT CADBURY CASTLE THAT THESE CELTIC BRITONS MADE A STAND AGAINST THE GERMANIC INVADERS.

A NEARBY VILLAGE...

...WAS BEING WATCHED.

A SAXON RAID!

THE SURVIVORS FLED...

...TO THE ONLY PLACE WHERE THEY KNEW THEY WOULD BE SAFE...

...THE HILL FORT AT CADBURY.

INSIDE THE FORT WERE KITCHENS, WORKSHOPS, AND HOMES FOR THE SOLDIERS AND LOCAL PEOPLE.

BUT WHO WAS THE FORT'S LORD? WHICH CHIEFTAIN WAS STRONG ENOUGH TO KEEP THE VARIOUS LOCAL TRIBES AND KIN GROUPS FROM FIGHTING EACH OTHER?

AT THE FORT'S CENTRE WAS THE GREAT HALL, AND INSIDE...

...SAT THE FORT'S CHIEFTAIN.

AFTER LISTENING TO THE VILLAGERS' STORY...

...THE CHIEFTAIN AND HIS TRIBAL CHIEFS AND CAPTAINS PLANNED THEIR COUNTER-ATTACK ON THE RAIDERS.

MANY PLACES IN BRITAIN HAVE CLAIMED TO BE ARTHUR'S CAMELOT. BUT ONLY ONE CAN BE THE TRUE SITE.

SADLY, THE LOCATION OF THE TRUE CAMELOT IS STILL HIDDEN BY THE PASSING OF TIME.

THE END

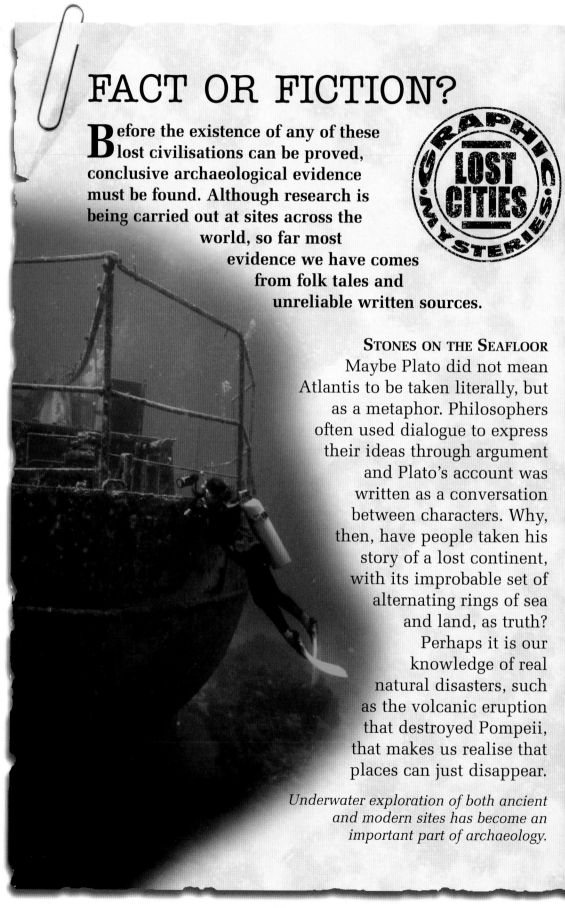

FACT OR FICTION?

Before the existence of any of these lost civilisations can be proved, conclusive archaeological evidence must be found. Although research is being carried out at sites across the world, so far most evidence we have comes from folk tales and unreliable written sources.

GRAPHIC MYSTERIES: LOST CITIES

STONES ON THE SEAFLOOR
Maybe Plato did not mean Atlantis to be taken literally, but as a metaphor. Philosophers often used dialogue to express their ideas through argument and Plato's account was written as a conversation between characters. Why, then, have people taken his story of a lost continent, with its improbable set of alternating rings of sea and land, as truth? Perhaps it is our knowledge of real natural disasters, such as the volcanic eruption that destroyed Pompeii, that makes us realise that places can just disappear.

Underwater exploration of both ancient and modern sites has become an important part of archaeology.

GOLD IN THE JUNGLE

The most interesting part of the El Dorado legend is that it is a European invention. A few years after Orellana's expedition, the Spanish returned to the Amazon in search of the kingdoms he described. They found nothing. Was Orellana lying to impress the Spanish court and find fame, like other explorers who had found civilisations in South America? Did his story become so famous just because it captured the imaginations of Europeans determined to find and exploit the wealth of the new world?

Could a South American king, like the one above, have held the key to El Dorado's secrets?

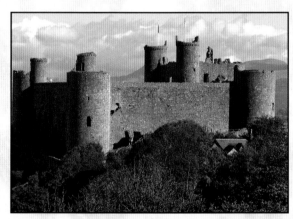

Could Camelot have looked like this? Harlech Castle in Wales (above) was built not long after the French poet, Chrétien de Troyes, first mentioned Camelot by name in the twelfth century.

THE AGE OF CHIVALRY?

If there was a real King Arthur, he would not have been the romantic hero we think of today. There was no medieval king named Arthur. He was more likely to have been a Celtic warlord living in the Dark Ages and he would not have lived in a grand palace, like the Camelot of legend. However, there is evidence at places like Cadbury, that an important leader like Arthur did once exist.

GLOSSARY

Angles Germanic people from Denmark who invaded Great Britain in the fifth and sixth centuries A.D.

archaeology The study of historical remains, such as relics.

barren A place that is bleak and or does not produce many crops.

Britons Native people in Great Britain at the time of the Romans.

chieftain A leader of a tribe or tribes.

chivalry Medieval knightly system that valued honouring and serving women and defending those in need of protection.

civil war A war between different groups from the same country.

civilisation A culture that has reached an advanced stage in social development.

colony Group of people originally from one country now occupying or ruling another territory on behalf of their homeland.

conclusive Evidence that is so strong that it puts an end to debate.

conquistadors Spanish conquerors of South America.

Dark Ages Period in European history, c. A.D. 500 until A.D. 1000, in which civilisation was said to be in decline.

enchanted To be influenced, controlled or dazzled by someone or something.

expedition A journey undertaken for a specific purpose.

exploit To unfairly make use of something or someone.

Inca The Quechuan people of Peru.

ingot An amount of metal moulded into a convenient shape.

Jutes Germanic people who invaded England and settled in Kent.

knight A soldier of noble birth who served his king.

manuscripts Ancient documents written by hand.

marvel To be surprised at something, often because of its beauty.

medieval Historical period in Europe from c. A.D. 1000 to A.D. 1500.

monastery An enclosed community where monks live and work.

mortal Describes any living thing that will eventually die.

philosopher A person who seeks wisdom or knowledge. The word philosophy means 'love of knowledge'.

plain A large area of country that has no trees.

Pompeii A city in southwest Italy that was destroyed by an eruption of the volcano Vesuvius in A.D. 79.

Roman legion The principal unit of the Roman army containing 5,000 men.

Saxons Germanic tribe that conquered England in the ninth century.

skiff A small, flat-bottomed rowing boat.

FOR MORE INFORMATION

FOR FURTHER READING
If you liked this book, you might also want to try:

Where was Atlantis?
by Brian Innes, Steck-Vaughn 1999

Atlantis: The Lost City?
by Andrew Donkin, DK Publishing 2000

King Arthur and the Knights of the Round Table
by Marcia Williams, Walker Books 1997

Terror on the Amazon: The Quest for El Dorado
by Phil Gates, DK Publishing 2000

Exploring the World of King Arthur
by Christopher Snyder, Thames and Hudson 2000

The Mystery of Atlantis
by Chris Oxlade and Anita Ganeri, Heinemann Library 2000

INDEX

Web Sites

Due to the changing nature of Internet links, the Salariya Book Company has developed an online list of Web sites related to the subject of this book. This site is updated regularly. Please use this link to access the list:

http://www.book-house.co.uk/grmy/aolc